a rebellious nature

poems by john clark vincent

cover and interior design by lisa d. holmes
(yulan studio, yulanstudio.com)

published in portland, oregon by yulan studio
printed in the united states

first edition
isbn: 979-8-9863990-3-4

... for butterflies everywhere

acknowledgements

my sincere gratitude to my wife, lisa d. holmes (yulan studio),
for designing and publishing this manuscript (and for so many
other reasons), and to linda bybee kapfer, waka t. brown,
cheryl duffy, riley glissendorf, matteo merenda, aileen sheedy,
paulann petersen, and klara kjome fischer for their inspiration,
feedback, support, and friendship.

contents

sensing humor 9

unlikely as it seems 10

moving on 11

times such as these 12

nothing left to say 13

dark blue afternoon 15

talking with a bro 16

buried by syntax 17

reasons to drink less 19

waiting for the parade to pass 20

browsing the used idea shop 21

uncertainty 22

petals and leaves 23

kindnesses 24

becoming 25

breaking trail 26

making choices 27

character actors 28

learning to laugh at myself 29

solstice for old people 30

letting go 31

becoming the path 32

the life we live 34

waiting it out 35

ode to a butterfly 36

a rebellious nature 37

sensing humor

november's easy
   breeze releases leaves
      of birch and black
         tupelo vibrantly yellow
      and orange to drift
   without intention
      to the path i
         still sweep;
            not to mock
         but to
      remind there
         is no end
            to the falling,
      to the breeze,
   to the trees,
      to the path
         itself...

unlikely as it seems

were dawn and twilight to meet
they'd be such fast and forever friends,

instantly bound by their love of
sheer wonder... and of dreams.

for dawn feels dreams like no other
and twilight, well,

twilight still remembers them,
and recognizes their bittersweet beauty

in the eyes of dawn's stunning light
and in the embers twilight continues to nurse.

midday and late afternoon would no doubt
roll their eyes then get back to work, but

dawn would continue sharing all her hope while
twilight puts on a kettle and leans in to listen...

moving on

late autumn's leaves need no
eulogy, no
obituary to help them be
remembered.

they've said their goodbyes;
used up their
paint; achieved their lifelong
desire to fly.

their year is done. their tree has
fallen asleep.
so they snuggle together to
listen and wait,

knowing some brand new
dream will
come for them. some new job
will begin.

times such as these

there are moments when
butterflies break my heart.

moments when i cannot bear to hear the
words i sense they are not speaking.

and because there are so few,
what songs they sing are given
to the breeze and
brush of grass, swaying, lost in thought.

i cannot bear to watch them weave
the stories their children may not hear.

then i wonder,
will children even exist next year?
and if they do,
will fear
or love
mark those tender beginnings?

that i cannot know, but
even so,
on warm and easy afternoons,
when i cannot have it any other way,
eyes downcast,
listening as i breathe,
i want to believe
it could be love.

nothing left to say

you're just sad, he said. it's hard to
be reminded that we're all alone.
you're alone, and i'm alone too.
we all are. you
do realize that don't you?

i just sat there with my coffee and
my keyboard and my blank screen,
missing all the words that had been
coming round to see me so regularly i
had started to believe they'd
come to stay.

until today, i answered, *i might have*
laughed at you because i knew, or
at least i believed,
those words loved me. i
thought they understood what was
in my heart.

they did, he said, *or they*
wouldn't have lingered at all.
you know how words are.
they're capable of love, but they
are words after all.
they have so much to do.
you can't expect them to
stay with only you, right?

i know, i said, *but i loved them.*
i still love them. i've been

writing them over and over and i
understand i can't keep doing that.
it's just so quiet now.

then let it be quiet, he said.
remember what they told you.
think how they made you feel.
and, when you can,
let them go and pick up your pen.

dark blue afternoon

the tea in my cup
     first warms my hands,
               wrapped around the
               chinese porcelain. then
    warms my nose and
fogs my glasses as,
     eyes closed,
             i breathe it in. again.
             i breathe it in again,
    cup resting heavily against my
chin as, head bowed and eyes
    still closed i hear the
             percussionist brush his snares while
             the bass slows time and
    the sax player remembers how it felt
to lose everything. i
    breathe it in again then
             tip the cup to let it in,
             sharp and free as only
    tea can be. peppermint. from the
blue pot out front. scent still
    lingering on my fingers.
             it's the shit and i
             love the way it
    helps me feel so
utterly safe and alone.

talking with a bro

lao tzu said,
be like water.

       dude, that's the thing...
       be, like, you know,
       water. be water.
       that's what the universe
       acts like. is like.

       that's what life is. that's
       what it does, bro.
       flows out into
       empty spaces. like,
       water.

       just flow with it.
       find a channel, then
       go for a ride.

       circle into a sweet little
       bay, then stay,
       at least for a while.

oh, and...
keep breathing.

buried by syntax

for a while,
i think she loved the
idea of me, even if
she never cared to know
the real me.

so i wondered, if i
enrolled in this course and
lived my life as
an idea,
could i find some
happiness there?

looking back,
i don't remember many
easy smiles,
but the lack of reality
i remember quite well.

because life as fantasy
slowly sucks us in.
it grabs hold ankle high,
grips tight and
slowly, inexorably, pulls.

first we lose our footing, then
little by little
day by day
year after year,

our souls begin to sink away.

i tried to show her that
through my actions, like
finding a therapist who
reminded me of thoreau; and
booking business flights that
required longer stays; and
mixing xanax with my whiskey.

but,
she wasn't a verb person.
she was prone to
declarations.

it was mostly past tense with her.
"i didn't like that."
except when the future grew tense,
"i'm not looking forward to that."

i came to think of things in
terms of tense.
everything was tense
all the time, until our
morphological lives grew
too complex to puctuate at all.

eventually i dropped that class.
i mean i
felt bad about not finishing,
but the lessons i learned have
proven invaluable.

reasons to drink less

alcohol is a guru that sets you free.
that part's true.

it loosens the rope that holds your baggage on your back
and allows a little pain to pool upon the carpet.

but it doesn't work for free.
you always pay.

you pay until you're upside down in debt but
can't remember how you got there.

so what i'm saying is
there are other gurus to consider.

and while all of them charge something,
the payment plans vary immensely.

some are easy to live with and offer a totally chill lifestyle.
some allow you to believe everything's actually perfect already.

waiting for the parade to pass

the dust i brush from the books that helped me
shape the dreams i dream
reminds me how long i've waited to begin the journey
i keep promising myself.

but action requires planning, i've always said,
and planning takes time.

but how much time is actually required to
turn a page or begin a new chapter?
how much time to simply pick a book up and
try to remember what brought us together in the first place?

was it a happy story at a sad time? or could it have been
a fragment from someone else's vision—
someone else's promise to someone else's heart —
that i was somehow trying to feel for myself,
trying to believe could be my promise to my heart...

a promise now covered with the dust of a timid life,
sitting on a shelf in the corner of a room
i cannot bring myself to leave.

browsing the used idea shop

old ideas,
like votive candles,
only burn so long before

they melt away
or their misshapen remains
get stored alongside other good intentions.

but frankly,
i don't believe i'm
quite ready to give them all up.

so here i am,
hoping some of those ideas
still hold the truth i once felt, and

like votive cups
discovered in an attic drawer,
opaque with dust and dried wax,

they might
consider allowing me
to maybe clean them up and try again.

uncertainty

love has come and gone,
yet my heart remains awake...
breathlessly awake,
listening for the soft sounds
of rose petals as they fall.

petals and leaves

petals aren't always precious, you know.
and neither are leaves. i mean,
they have their moments… times when
you see them smiling from ear to ear as it were.

but then they fade like all replaceable parts fade.
they shine until they don't anymore.
that's just how life is.

they have their moment. then it's like
they take a long, slow, reflective walk, and
it occurs to them there's a fall in their future—
they will lose all they have come to love.

it's easy to see the sorrow in their expressions, as
they lay beneath the monuments they helped build.

and the way they shrink into themselves—the way they
decompose right before your eyes makes people
hate them. makes people go to a lot of trouble to simply
avoid them if they can. because who needs that mess. but,

petals are just being petals. and leaves are just being leaves.

kindnesses

it's when you forget me that you set me free.
but till that day arrives, here i'll be, willingly captive,

daily bowing to the bonds we shall never see, but with
occasional uncertainty, we lovingly weave.

i will provide kindnesses where and when i can.
i will scrub away the stains of life's smaller sorrows,

and promise that when i go, though stains may remain,
what sorrows i can gather i shall stuff into my pockets.

becoming

... for lisa

we have
        been lovers
                for years

yet so
        little time
                has passed

since we
        (both of us)
                emerged

from dreams
        we called
                our lives,

having learned
        to breathe
                together...

breaking trail

life knows itself well, as it should.
it's certainly had the time to
recognize its tendencies—its

habit of going around the wall until
the wall says fuck you one time
too many, so life just pushes through.

life can't help wondering what
lies ahead; what, if anything, is
out there. what hasn't it experienced?

and so it flows forth, carrying us all
along with it, like a mother who
is addicted to something she

hasn't found—at least not yet. a
mother who eats her children when
she must... when it's the only way

to save them. because she knows they
will still be with her, and they will
remember the lessons she has learned

as she searched, as she failed, as she
finally found a way through, as she shaped
her own reality, and left a trail to follow.

making choices

life allows us to choose our
own path, which is to say,
it lets us decide how we feel
about the path it puts us on.

so be decisive, but keep your
mind open and your heart
awake, for we are the eyes of
life, and we learn together.

with a closer look we may see that
love is everywhere. sometimes
in the open, but more often
hiding, or lingering, or benignly

wondering if any eyes will find it,
if any hearts will open to let it in,
if any souls will choose to mingle
with the essence of its being.

character actors

love stories are the best...

stories that have us
drowning in love and
loving it...

stories that call us into the
wild world and teach us
how to share the breath
all others breathe...

stories that help us
rest in solitude until we're
surprised into happiness by a
moment we then treasure.

character actors all,
we consume the roles that
consume us, and,
every single time,

love stories are the best.

learning to laugh at myself

the perfect notion—the ideal—does not exist in the real.
there's no natural feel to that view of life.
because ideals are often carved with a knife.

we cut out the parts we can't understand,
then paint over the scars with glitter and stars.
we scrub away the dark spots.
we lie to ourselves for as long as it takes.

when i accepted the truth in that,
the nearly perfect pain i felt was real enough for me.
i mean, the truth is always there to see.
i simply chose to look away; or to pretend each blossom's
brief ecstatic fever dream could happen every day;

conveniently forgetting how hard it was to become a flower at all,
forgetting the late frost or early freeze that took so many friends away.
forgetting that evening comes for more than just the light.
it also throws friendly shade on perfectly planned afternoons.

solstice for old people

at the end of things, we're left with
mostly empty pockets. nothing much to
give that anyone still desires.

there are memories, of course…
but they've become images that even
we don't really need anymore.

and having spent our lives wholly disinterested
in merely keeping busy, now is not the
time to develop mindless hobbies.

there are, of course, the lives of those we
know. those we love. but the lives to be lived
are theirs. they will be fine on their own.

so how do we find real purpose once
we've fallen so far behind that people have
forgotten we were even running the race?

honestly, it appears to me we don't. so the best we
can do is move to the outer lanes, watch our pulse,
then step off the track when it's time to call it.

letting go

the essence of eternity, for each of us,
is that to which we give ourselves till nothing's left.

it's the path we travel till we become the path.
it's the energy flow we flow into.

essence forever becoming,
yet lasting the briefest of moments.

time does not come to mind...

becoming the path

nurse logs once lived a vibrant life.
each day for years they'd
reach for the light and more often than not,
touch it. feel it in their
gnarled bark.

now they garden.
not an easy hobby for big timber to
undertake. but,
beginnings are rarely easy.

at first the logs just lay around,
no longer swaying.
they're done with the wind and,
deep down, they know it.
time now is spent in repose,
reflecting on sunrises that suddenly seem
even more special.

but as time passes, they learn to
help young plants breathe.
and now,
plants of every type tumble across the
fading reality of these bundles of
broken bark and sagging wood.

the once disenchanted logs become a
playground filled with
ferns, flowers, lichen and the sweetest
baby trees.

they do it for love.
and though it makes them sad to
watch what they no longer can become,
they hope to learn what life can be
when one is not a tree.

the life we live

we live as we're taught
until life touches our heart.
it is then the life
we are meant to live begins,
with joy and pain intertwined.

waiting it out

a week's worth of ice runs down the
gutters from the roof, across the
driveway, then the sidewalk, to
empty at the edge of the street.

two tiny birds appear at the public bath—
the one next to the blue buddha—
chattering to one another as though they
had been holding it in for days.

one of them found the experience so
heavenly she lingered in the water till
her toes began to wrinkle.

ode to a butterfly

can we own the love
we feel, call it our own, or
must we set it free
for it to remember the
heart that watched its wings unfold...

a rebellious nature

i've grown so old that
most of my memories
lay buried in boxes i stack in
various closets.

many of them dead already,
a few barely breathe as i
puzzle them into a
nearly recognizable form.

but i still savor the scars of
each moment that etched its intention
into the lining of my heart,
then spray painted its name on
the walls of my imagination.